Believe

in your vision.

Whose Shoes Are YOU WEARING?

2020

TRANSFORMATIONAL

Planner

SIMPLIFY, SET & TAKE ACTION
TO SMASH YOUR GOALS!

6TH EDITION | A 12-MONTH GUIDE BASED ON THE BOOK BY
CHRISTINE K. ST. VIL & JULIAN B. KIGANDA

FEATURING GOAL-SETTING STRATEGIES, SUCCESS TIPS,
AND INSPIRING STORIES FROM 12 DYNAMIC WOMEN

KKULA
MEDIA

KKULA MEDIA   WASHINGTON, DC   2019

welcome!

We're Christine St. Vil and Julian B. Kiganda—two sisters who have traveled a long, winding path to uncover and walk in our purpose. Ever since releasing our book in 2014, we have received powerful testimonials from women and men alike about how *Whose Shoes Are You Wearing? 12 Steps to Uncovering the Woman You Really Want to Be* has helped them uncover what has kept them from pursuing their dreams. So we developed this planner to help you do just that: put some deadlines on your dreams. But first, you've got to set some goals. Here are our ABC's of goal-setting:

A – Affirm & Define

- Affirm who you are at your core.
- Write down what you're passionate about.
- Determine the activities that come naturally to you and bring you joy.

B – Believe & Visualize

- Believe what you don't see.
- Write your vision down on paper.
- Create a vision board or binder.

C – Create & Take Action

- Create a strategy and write it down.
- Put a deadline on your action steps.

Create community for accountability. (*Join our exclusive Whose Shoes Next Level Transformation Facebook group*: bit.ly/wsbnextlevel)

HOW TO ACHIEVE
your goals

We know how setting goals can sometimes seem overwhelming and complex. Throughout this planner, we've included success tips to help you simplify the process and stay motivated. In addition, we've outlined an approach below to help you successfully set and achieve your goals.

1. First, gain *clarity* and *commit* to your vision for this year.

2. Understand that goals are the building blocks which allow you to achieve your vision. Once you set your goals, they should stay the same for the year. However, don't be afraid to pivot if and when necessary.

3. Determine the #1 thing that needs to happen to make each goal a reality. Focus on getting that one thing done.

4. Each goal you set must be based on:
   - your ability to fulfill the requirements of each goal,
   - having the right team with the right skills to help you complete each task,
   - having or knowing where to find the resources (tools, materials, capital) needed to complete the required tasks,
   - and having enough time to accomplish each goal.

5. If any of the above conditions don't exist, find a way to bring them into existence. *Don't be afraid to think beyond the obvious. Get creative.*

6. Once you've established your goals are doable, you're now ready to determine the *actions* you must take to complete each goal. Plan your work. Work your plan. And . . .

7. Take action. *Let's get it done in 2020!*

MY *vision* FOR 2020

Write out your vision for the year below. Be bold, be creative, and be about getting it done this year!

_____

_____

_____

_____

_____

_____

_____

_____

_____

_____

_____

_____

_____

_____

_____

_____

_____

_____

MY BIG *goals*

Your goals for the year should be based on your vision. They will help you focus your actions and prioritize how you spend your time every month. What are your goals—personal and/or professional—for 2020?

(Note: It's okay to have less than five goals for the year. Do you!)

1. _____

_____

_____

2. _____

_____

_____

3. _____

_____

_____

4. _____

_____

_____

5. _____

_____

_____

MY  *why*

It's so easy to give up on your dream when it feels like you're not making progress. That's why it's so important to be clear about *why* achieving your goals matters to you. Your "why" will keep you going when you think you have nothing left in you. *What's your "why"?* (You may have more than one.)

_____

_____

_____

_____

_____

_____

_____

_____

_____

_____

_____

_____

_____

_____

_____

_____

_____

MY  vision board

Create your mini vision board on these pages, choosing words and images to visually paint the picture of the year you want to have. There are no limits to what you can envision!

You are Light

Your vision becomes your thoughts.
Your thoughts become your words.
Your words become your actions.
Your actions become your reality.

2020 is the year of vision. And with vision, comes light.

Don't allow anyone to dim your light.

The world needs you.

Even when you're feeling alone, you are not alone.

Read these words until you believe them for yourself.

You matter.

Your. Life. Matters.

Your past mistakes do not define you, they only make you stronger.

Beautiful Queen, you are more than what's on the surface.

You are light to someone else's darkness.

You are happiness to someone else's sadness.

You are magnificent, just the way God created you to be.

—CHRISTINE ST. VIL

JANUARY

ronnisha wilson

Founder, Demosea'
@demoseabotanicals

As a young girl growing up in one the most impoverished and violent areas in Los Angeles, all I ever wanted to do was change my circumstances. I knew the way to do that was through education.

I put constant pressure on myself to achieve. I knew I had to go into the medical field because it paid well. I didn't care that it wasn't my passion. It wasn't until my life was shaken up, that I would start to reevaluate my path.

I was on my way to college to study business marketing when I was diagnosed with two autoimmune disorders: psoriasis, which causes skin cells to renew too quickly, resulting in a red, scaly rash on the skin; and psoriatic arthritis, which causes inflammation that leads to swelling, pain, fatigue and stiff joints. As a young woman, the physical toll this disorder took on my body was devastating, but the hit my mental health took was worse. The constant pressure I put on myself achieve to my goals led to chronic anxiety.

continued on page 16

Get it done

Review your vision and goals to make sure your
actions this month align with the results you want.

ACTION	RESULTS
1.	
2.	
3.	

JANUARY

S	M	T	W
			1
5	6	7	8
12	13	14	15
19	20	21	22
26	27	28	29

Desire to inspire. Use your purpose to transform the world.

−RONNISHA WILSON   #whoseshoes20

Th	F	S
2	3	4
9	10	11
16	17	18
23	24	25
30	31	

IMPORTANT DATES

1 New Year's Day

20 Martin Luther King, Jr. Holiday

_____
_____
_____
_____
_____
_____
_____
_____

DECEMBER 2019

S	M	T	W	T	F	S
1	2	3	4	5	6	7
8	9	10	11	12	13	14
15	16	17	18	19	20	21
22	23	24	25	26	27	28
29	30	31				

FEBRUARY 2020

S	M	T	W	T	F	S
						1
2	3	4	5	6	7	8
9	10	11	12	13	14	15
16	17	18	19	20	21	22
23	24	25	26	27	28	29

continued from page 12

I later found out that stress and anxiety was a huge trigger for my psoriasis and psoriatic arthritis flare ups. To add insult to injury, the medicine the doctors gave me to combat the physical symptoms of the disease was making matters worse. My skin suffered from hypopigmentation that led to hyperpigmentation.

Being proactive, I researched everything about the medicine that I was on and was alarmed. In my research, I learned that everything in my medication and the products I used was causing more harm than good. They were filled with harsh ingredients and chemicals that were causing burns and hypo- and hyperpigmentation.

I decided to make my own products using all natural ingredients. My circumstances and struggles led me to my passion and, ultimately, my purpose. Creating products for women of color with pure botanical oils and all natural ingredients that they do not have to second guess is my passion. My purpose in life is to use my platform to empower, inspire and help women heal through self-care and wellness.

Today, Demosea'—the company I created from my own personal struggle—is helping other women with theirs. When this entrepreneurial journey gets tough, I remember these women's stories and the impact my business has had on their lives. It is blessing to be able to bless others. It gives me the motivation to keep going.

SUCCESS *Tips*

1. BE PERSISTENT: A distinguishing attribute of those who succeed versus those who don't is persistence. You want to succeed? Keep going.

2. DON'T BE AFRAID TO PIVOT: Sometimes success is waiting for you on the other side of change. Turn the challenge of change into opportunity.

3. REMEMBER YOU OWE YOU: Give yourself and your business the same effort that you give the world. You are responsible for your own success. No one can stop you but you!

january
SUCCESSES

1. _____
   _____
   _____

2. _____
   _____
   _____

3. _____
   _____
   _____

What I learned: _____
_____
_____
_____

How I'll celebrate my success: _____
_____
_____
_____

NOTES

_____

_____

_____

_____

_____

_____

_____

_____

_____

_____

_____

_____

_____

_____

_____

_____

_____

_____

_____

_____

_____

_____

NOTES

_____

_____

_____

_____

_____

_____

_____

_____

_____

_____

_____

_____

_____

_____

_____

_____

_____

_____

_____

_____

_____

_____

_____

NOTES

_____

_____

_____

_____

_____

_____

_____

_____

_____

_____

_____

_____

_____

_____

_____

_____

_____

_____

_____

_____

_____

_____

_____

_____

FEBRUARY

amber valentine

Co-Founder and Creator,
Scale The Limit
@scalethelimit

My life-altering moment came in my mid-30s and rocked my whole world. I was very successful in my career, had a husband, 2.5 kids, and the white picket fence. Even though I had checked all the boxes I thought would make me happy, I was still miserable.

The one area of my life that no matter how hard I tried to fix I couldn't was my weight. I had struggled for 15 years with an extra 90 pounds and had recently been told I was morbidly obese at the doctors office. I was so frustrated that this one thing was so hard when I had been able to overcome so many other obstacles in my life. It was my therapist who changed my life

continued on page 26

Get it done

Review your vision and goals to make sure your
actions this month align with the results you want.

ACTION	RESULTS
1.	
2.	
3.	

FEBRUARY

S	M	T	W
2	3	4	5
9	10	11	12
16	17	18	19
23	24	25	26

If you can't spend ten minutes alone with yourself, who else is going to want to? Learn to love YOU. —AMBER VALENTINE   #whoseshoes20

Th	F	S
		1
6	7	8
13	14	15
20	21	22
27	28	29

IMPORTANT DATES

14 Valentine's Day
17 Presidents Day
26 Ash Wednesday

_____
_____
_____
_____
_____
_____
_____
_____
_____
_____

JANUARY 2020

S	M	T	W	T	F	S
			1	2	3	4
5	6	7	8	9	10	11
12	13	14	15	16	17	18
19	20	21	22	23	24	25
26	27	28	29	30	31	

MARCH 2020

S	M	T	W	T	F	S
1	2	3	4	5	6	7
8	9	10	11	12	13	14
15	16	17	18	19	20	21
22	23	24	25	26	27	28
29	30	31				

continued from page 22

forever. She pointed out that sometimes weight is an emotional barrier, that I may have had an underlying fear in my life which caused it to hold on. She suggested that because I had been raised in an abusive household, there was a possible fear of being desirable—a fear that becoming skinny may put me in danger.

Armed with that new knowledge, I put in the work to overcome that fear and to heal. I started meditating, visualizing, and using affirmations every morning to change my internal thoughts around my weight. I also created an awesome diet plan designed just for me. Along the journey I realized I had piled years of achievements into a life that was really designed for someone else.

In addition to I losing more than 70 pounds in just four months, I had some spiritual weight that had to go as well. I let go of the weight in my career and my relationships. Now I get to step on stage to motivate and inspire other women with my story of transformation. I speak on how I overcame: being raised in an abusive household, having a teen pregnancy, surviving a brush with homelessness, navigating the world with a tenth grade education—and *still* came out on top!

My story of internal, external and eternal transformation is helping others let go of their spiritual and physical weight, learn to love themselves unapologetically, and design their own happiness. I'm finally walking in shoes that fit me *perfectly*.

SUCCESS *Tips*

1. DEFEND YOUR GIFTS at all costs! You have something very special and its important that the world gets to see it.

2. STAND STILL FOR A MINUTE. We move so fast sometimes we forget that no matter what happens we already have what we really need.

3. YOU ARE SO MUCH MORE THAN ENOUGH.

february
SUCCESSES

1. _____

2. _____

3. _____

What I learned: _____

How I'll celebrate my success: _____

NOTES

NOTES

_____

_____

_____

_____

_____

_____

_____

_____

_____

_____

_____

_____

_____

_____

_____

_____

_____

_____

_____

_____

_____

_____

_____

_____

_____

NOTES

Believe in your purpose.

MARCH

topia tessema

Founder, Abiyah Naturals
@abiyah_naturals

I've always had the desire to help others see themselves and recognize their beauty inside and out. That journey first led me to become a social worker. In this role, I primarily supported women who were parenting children alone while trying to overcome obstacles; obstacles that were the result of generational struggles and expectations that society had placed on them. My mantra for them was always to realize that they had the God-given strength within them to overcome anything. I believed in these women wholeheartedly and kept that passion and drive in all my years of practice.

Life has a funny way of preparing you for what is to come. In 2011, I embarked on my own journey of single parenthood and gave birth to a beautiful baby girl. It hasn't been an easy journey, but my faith in God and the support and strength I received from my mother helped see me through. The very same words that I empowered my clients with over the

continued on page 36

Review your vision and goals to make sure your
actions this month align with the results you want.

ACTION	RESULTS
1.	
2.	
3.	

MARCH

S	M	T	W
1	2	3	4
8	9	10	11
15	16	17	18
22	23	24	25
29	30	31	

Anything is possible with God!   –TOPIA TESSEMA

#whoseshoes20

Th	F	S
5	6	7
12	13	14
19	20	21
26	27	28

IMPORTANT DATES

8 International Women's Day

8 Daylight Saving Time (Start)

17 St. Patrick's Day

19 Spring Begins

_____
_____
_____
_____
_____
_____
_____
_____

FEBRUARY 2020

S	M	T	W	T	F	S
						1
2	3	4	5	6	7	8
9	10	11	12	13	14	15
16	17	18	19	20	21	22
23	24	25	26	27	28	29

APRIL 2020

S	M	T	W	T	F	S
			1	2	3	4
5	6	7	8	9	10	11
12	13	14	15	16	17	18
19	20	21	22	23	24	25
26	27	28	29	30		

continued from page 32

years forced me to practice what I preached.

I decided to leave traditional social work because I knew that I would be limited if I continued to work for someone else. I was eventually led to use my gifts and my love for handmade natural body care products to start my own business, naming it Abiyah Naturals. I feel as if it has allowed me to do my social work in alternate way. My goal was to show others that you can use the gifts and skills you have to overcome your struggles and provide for your family.

As much as I love what I do, being an entrepreneur has come with its own set of challenges. Many ideas I thought would work didn't. When they fell apart, by the grace of God, something better came along. I've come to learn that as one door closes, another one opens. It opens because I did not have fear or sadness about that first door closing.

I now understand that my business has allowed me to fully walk in my purpose. At the very root of its beginnings—the transitions, ups and downs, and even the products I make by hand—building my business has shown me that all things come to fruition through a process. Trust the process in all things.

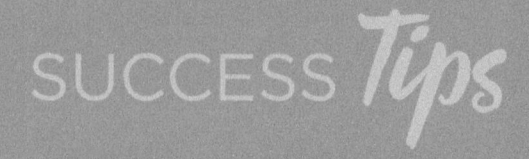

SUCCESS *Tips*

1. BELIEVE IN YOUR GIFTS and abilities.

2. FORGIVE YOURSELF AND OTHERS for the things that may have happened so that you can have what is meant for you. Know you are worthy and worth it!

3. UNDERSTAND THAT ALL THINGS TAKE TIME AND PATIENCE.

march
SUCCESSES

1. _____
   _____
   _____

2. _____
   _____
   _____

3. _____
   _____
   _____

What I learned: _____
_____
_____
_____

How I'll celebrate my success: _____
_____
_____
_____

NOTES

NOTES

NOTES

APRIL

quniana futrell

Children's Champion
ECE Firm, LLC
@authorqfutrell

Ironically, I discovered my purpose after being terminated from what I thought was my dream job working as a director of a child care on a naval base.

With all my belongings from my now former office in hand, I walked to my car in front of my staff as if I had done something wrong. After climbing to the top of what I thought was my ladder of success, I was now being publicly humiliated, feeling betrayed by those I had trusted. I began questioning God, asking daily, "How could you let this happen to me?" As I watched many who wronged me rise, I felt ashamed and rejected.

As resilient as I was, this was an very difficult time for me. From this pain, I was forced to sit still and listen. In that stillness I found my purpose and discovered I was created to help others change their story and heal from their "momma trauma." My own trauma had come from growing up with two parents who were incarcerated.

continued on page 46

Get it done

Review your vision and goals to make sure your
actions this month align with the results you want.

ACTION	RESULTS
1.	
2.	
3.	

APRIL

S	M	T	W
			1
5	6	7	8
12	13	14	15
19	20	21	22
26	27	28	29

Change the family, change the world!

– QUNIANA FUTRELL   #whoseshoes20

Th	F	S
2	3	4
9	10	11
16	17	18
23	24	25
30		

IMPORTANT DATES

1 April Fool's Day
5 Palm Sunday
9 Passover
12 Easter Sunday
22 Earth Day

_____
_____
_____
_____
_____
_____
_____
_____
_____

MARCH 2020

S	M	T	W	T	F	S
1	2	3	4	5	6	7
8	9	10	11	12	13	14
15	16	17	18	19	20	21
22	23	24	25	26	27	28
29	30	31				

MAY 2020

S	M	T	W	T	F	S
					1	2
3	4	5	6	7	8	9
10	11	12	13	14	15	16
17	18	19	20	21	22	23
24/31	25	26	27	28	29	30

continued from page 42

I learned to tap into my inner champion and make the decision to trust God. I had to believe that the "thank you, but no thank you" letters I received during my job hunt meant that I wasn't supposed to work there, not that they were rejecting me. I now understand that had I not been rejected by so many, I would've settled for less than I deserved.

Romans 8:28 helped me to see the good in my situation: "All things work together for the good of those who love [God] and are called to His purpose." I had to believe that God had more for me. I had to also be willing to forgive my absent parents and even myself. I knew that holding on to unforgiveness and bitterness would prevent me from leaving my legacy. This has now become my formula for winning the fight for my life and continuing to change my story for the next generation.

I am now a best-selling author, serial entrepreneur, award-winning philanthropist, and most recently, a film maker. I have created an international movement called, Why My Mom© where I want the world to shout "Trauma Ain't Normal®." The goal is to stop normalizing trauma and help families heal so we can raise healthy children and break painful generational cycles. Our agency, the ECE Firm, LLC, even created a curriculum for prisons called, Parenting Behind Bars©. I now travel and speak on what it takes to build champions. Although these shoes now fit, they aren't always comfortable—but I wouldn't have it any other way!

SUCCESS *Tips*

1. If you can have a doctor for every other pain of your body, get one for your mind. THERAPY IS NORMAL.

2. In business, DO WHAT YOUR CUSTOMERS WANT, not what you like.

3. SUCCESS EQUALS SACRIFICE!

april SUCCESSES

1. _____
_____
_____

2. _____
_____
_____

3. _____
_____
_____

What I learned: _____
_____
_____
_____

How I'll celebrate my success: _____
_____
_____
_____

NOTES

NOTES

NOTES

MAY

kimberly d. sumpter

Host of the Sistahs
Connect Podcast
@sistahsconnect

The universe moves when you move. That's the revelation
that I was open to receiving this year after I decided to step
away from fear, doubt, and insecurity, and walked boldly
into my purpose. I admit that I was my own worst enemy at
times. Although I was clear on what it was that made me feel
the most fulfilled, I was too afraid to take a leap of faith and
pursue what really me happy. I was afraid of failing or being
seen as a failure.

Last year, I finally made a decision walk away from
my 9-to-5 job doing medical billing to pursue my dream

continued on page 56

Get it done

Review your vision and goals to make sure your
actions this month align with the results you want.

ACTION	RESULTS
1.	
2.	
3.	

MAY

S	M	T	W
3	4	5	6
10	11	12	13
17	18	19	20
24 ⎯⎯⎯ 31	25	26	27

If you have to sacrifice anything in life, make sure it's not your peace. —KIMBERLY D. SUMPTER   #whoseshoes20

Th	F	S
	1	2
7	8	9
14	15	16
21	22	23
28	29	30

IMPORTANT DATES

10 Mother's Day
25 Memorial Day

_____
_____
_____
_____
_____
_____
_____
_____

APRIL 2020

S	M	T	W	T	F	S
			1	2	3	4
5	6	7	8	9	10	11
12	13	14	15	16	17	18
19	20	21	22	23	24	25
26	27	28	29	30		

JUNE 2020

S	M	T	W	T	F	S
	1	2	3	4	5	6
7	8	9	10	11	12	13
14	15	16	17	18	19	20
21	22	23	24	25	26	27
28	29	30				

continued from page 52

of becoming a full time entrepreneur and to launch my podcast. I went through the motions by handing in my resignation and telling everyone of my big plans. I was finally ready. Or was I?

Within a few short weeks fear turned into panic which led me to secure another job. I was now sitting at my new desk, in a new work environment desperately wanting to feel as though I made the right decision. What I was really experiencing was a feeling of disappointment in myself and regret. How did I allow fear to order my steps?

About eight months later, I was driving to work one morning and a sense of peace came over me. I felt that it was God telling me that there was a bigger plan for my life. In that moment, my fear shifted into fearlessness. I thanked God for giving me the courage and peace so that I could be free to move in the direction of my destiny. To do that, I had to leave the negative self talk behind. I then took a serious look at my finances and saved more than I spent. I also made a promise to myself that no matter how tough things got, I would no longer operate in a spirit of fear and I would *never* give up.

Today I am a full time entrepreneur building my candle business (Wax Kandy Candle Co.). I have also chosen to use my voice to empower, celebrate and inspire women of color through my Sistahs Connect podcast. I'm finally walking in my purpose and have no plans to look back; I know that God has ordered my steps to move forward.

SUCCESS *Tips*

1. CULTIVATE A CIRCLE OF SISTER FRIENDS that support and honor one another, then cherish and nurture those friendships.

2. F.E.A.R. IS FALSE EVIDENCE APPEARING REAL so don't let it stop you from moving into your purpose. You have to believe with all your heart that you are destined and equipped to do great things.

3. When it comes to business, always UNDER PROMISE AND OVER DELIVER.

may
SUCCESSES

1. _____
   _____
   _____

2. _____
   _____
   _____

3. _____
   _____
   _____

What I learned: _____
_____
_____
_____

How I'll celebrate my success: _____
_____
_____
_____

NOTES

_____
_____
_____
_____
_____
_____
_____
_____
_____
_____
_____
_____
_____
_____
_____
_____
_____
_____
_____
_____
_____
_____
_____
_____
_____
_____
_____
_____

NOTES

NOTES

JUNE

shawn clarke
Owner, Constant Covering LLC
@constantcovering

In 2014 I was let go from my job as an administrative assistant with no real explanation. To be honest, I was relieved because the environment I had been working in for two years was so toxic. I wasn't looking for another corporate job at the time and I certainly wasn't looking to start a business. I have always been a creative person; however, I never thought my hands would bring me to create a business of my own.

I leaned on my faith and meditated on Psalm 91:4, "He will cover you with His feathers, and under His wings you will find refuge; His faithfulness will be your shield and rampart." With that knowledge,

continued on page 66

Get it done

Review your vision and goals to make sure your
actions this month align with the results you want.

ACTION	RESULTS
1.	
2.	
3.	

JUNE

S	M	T	W
	1	2	3
7	8	9	10
14	15	16	17
21	22	23	24
28	29	30	

Treat others the way you want to be treated.

–SHAWN CLARKE   #whoseshoes20

Th	F	S
4	5	6
11	12	13
18	19	20
25	26	27

IMPORTANT DATES

21 Father's Day
20 Summer Begins

_____
_____
_____
_____
_____
_____
_____
_____

MAY 2020

S	M	T	W	T	F	S
					1	2
3	4	5	6	7	8	9
10	11	12	13	14	15	16
17	18	19	20	21	22	23
24/31	25	26	27	28	29	30

JULY 2020

S	M	T	W	T	F	S
			1	2	3	4
5	6	7	8	9	10	11
12	13	14	15	16	17	18
19	20	21	22	23	24	25
26	27	28	29	30	31	

continued from page 62

Constant Covering was born in April of 2015. I had just begun my own natural hair journey and wore many styles with my personal headwrap collection. I realized other women had a need for what I now call a "protective styling hack." We handmake pre-tied satin-lined headwraps and turbans for that woman on the go. Building this business has definitely come with its challenges.

Early on I was a one woman show and believed I could meet the demand of the consumer. I was sadly mistaken; my time frame for delivery was three to four weeks for an order! I eventually hired a seamstress and shortened that delivery time to three to seven *days*.

There are times when I receive a message from a mother who needed to transform quickly when she left home with her kids and my headwrap was a time-saver. Or a spouse whose wife is undergoing chemo becomes a customer and he tells me how beautiful his wife feels wearing my headwrap. These are the moments I know this is exactly what I should be doing.

Sometimes, as powerful women shouldering families, careers, and standing as the matriarchs of our communities, we forget the enormity of our responsibility and the toll it takes on our spirit. Be sure to call on your fellow Queens, while remembering to stay covered in the care of the Creator.

SUCCESS *Tips*

1. HAVE SUPERB CUSTOMER SERVICE: "treat others the way you want to be treated" is also true in business.

2. If you do not complete your to do list FORGIVE YOURSELF and push it to the next day.

3. LISTEN TO YOUR BODY: when it's time to rest be sure to rest

june
SUCCESSES

1. _____
   _____
   _____

2. _____
   _____
   _____

3. _____
   _____
   _____

What I learned: _____
_____
_____
_____

How I'll celebrate my success: _____
_____
_____
_____

NOTES

_____

_____

_____

_____

_____

_____

_____

_____

_____

_____

_____

_____

_____

_____

_____

_____

_____

_____

_____

_____

_____

_____

_____

_____

NOTES

NOTES

Believe in your power.

JULY

kimberly spruill

Author, Speaker
Workshop Facilitator
@gracedforpurpose5

I discovered my purpose after overcoming domestic abuse. I was almost strangled to death in my own living room by a man who was living with me. As traumatic and painful as that incident was, it was that very incident that pushed me into the will of God like never before. I had never consulted God about being in a relationship with this man who I was also intimate with. I eventually realized my feelings of loneliness and desire for companionship led me into this unhealthy relationship.

It made me understand the danger in stepping outside of God's will and the consequences that follow. During this time, I was at my lowest point in life. I was broken and felt so distant from God. I prayed to be delivered from this pain in order to truly discover my purpose.

continued on page 76

Get it done

Review your vision and goals to make sure your actions this month align with the results you want.

ACTION	RESULTS
1.	
2.	
3.	

JULY

S	M	T	W
			1
5	6	7	8
12	13	14	15
19	20	21	22
26	27	28	29

No matter how big or small, consult God in it all.

–KIMBERLY SPRUILL   #whoseshoes20

Th	F	S
2	3	4
9	10	11
16	17	18
23	24	25
30	31	

IMPORTANT DATES

4 Independence Day

_____
_____
_____
_____
_____
_____
_____
_____

JUNE 2020

S	M	T	W	T	F	S
		1	2	3	4	5	6
7	8	9	10	11	12	13
14	15	16	17	18	19	20
21	22	23	24	25	26	27
28	29	30				

AUGUST 2020

S	M	T	W	T	F	S
						1
2	3	4	5	6	7	8
9	10	11	12	13	14	15
16	17	18	19	20	21	22
$^{23}/_{30}$	$^{24}/_{31}$	25	26	27	28	29

continued from page 72

I was emotionally drained, overwhelmed with sadness, and confused as to how I found myself in this situation. Because I was too ashamed and embarrassed to tell anyone what had happened, I suffered needlessly in silence.

I overcame this low place by praying and reading the Bible like never before. I was willing to do whatever I had to do to get healed from my broken state. I even gave up television for three months! I understood that God was the only one who could heal me during my "wilderness experience." Although the wilderness felt like a lonely place, it was the place where God had my full attention. He helped me to forgive the man who had wronged me.

During this time, I discovered that my purpose was to help others discover their purpose. All of the reading and studying prepared me for the speaking engagements that began coming my way, even while still teaching full time in middle school. I also wrote my first book, *Graced for Purpose*.

I now share my story of overcoming domestic violence with young girls and women from all walks of life. I help them realize that in order to discover their purpose, they must deal with any hurt and pain from their past so they can embrace their future. Sharing my story has ultimately made me realize that my obedience is tied to someone's deliverance.

SUCCESS *Tips*

1. CONSULT GOD ABOUT EVERY DECISION YOU MAKE, especially when it comes to relationships.

2. KNOW YOUR WORTH.

3. UNDERSTAND THAT THERE IS MUCH TO LOSE when you are connected to the wrong person.

july SUCCESSES

1. _____
   _____
   _____

2. _____
   _____
   _____

3. _____
   _____
   _____

What I learned: _____
_____
_____

How I'll celebrate my success: _____
_____
_____
_____

NOTES

NOTES

NOTES

_____

_____

_____

_____

_____

_____

_____

_____

_____

_____

_____

_____

_____

_____

_____

_____

_____

_____

_____

_____

_____

_____

Believe.
no matter what.

AUGUST

adeola ariyo-enikanoselu

Founder and
Executive Director,
THE GEMZ
Chief Brand Officer,
AAE Consulting
@adeolainspires
@thegemzinc

I learned to walk in my shoes in my early 20s when I discovered I had the gifts of leadership, service, and empowering others to dream and achieve gigantic goals. Before that, I often focused on wanting to be more outspoken, more outgoing, and more extroverted because I felt that was one of the surest recipes for success. I thought any other personality type was more of a disadvantage.

But despite my quiet demeanor, I discovered I had a knack for helping other female entrepreneurs excel when I became an entrepreneur myself. This started me on the journey of being more confident in who I was. I often thought, "There must be something unique about me and I need to spend time discovering it."

continued on page 86

Get it done

Review your vision and goals to make sure your actions this month align with the results you want.

ACTION	RESULTS
1.	
2.	
3.	

AUGUST

S	M	T	W
2	3	4	5
9	10	11	12
16	17	18	19
23 / 30	24 / 31	25	26

Ask yourself today: are you living or existing?

-ADEOLA ARIYO-ENIKANOSELU   #whoseshoes20

Th	F	S
		1
6	7	8
13	14	15
20	21	22
27	28	29

IMPORTANT DATES

_____
_____
_____
_____
_____
_____
_____
_____
_____

JULY 2020

S	M	T	W	T	F	S
			1	2	3	4
5	6	7	8	9	10	11
12	13	14	15	16	17	18
19	20	21	22	23	24	25
26	27	28	29	30	31	

SEPTEMBER 2020

S	M	T	W	T	F	S
		1	2	3	4	5
6	7	8	9	10	11	12
13	14	15	16	17	18	19
20	21	22	23	24	25	26
27	28	29	30			

continued from page 82

I grew up as a very shy and reserved girl, though I excelled in school all the way through college. But I was never confident enough to speak in public unless I absolutely had to. With the help of a few mentors who were very supportive, I was able to navigate my young adult years. That experience inspired me to launch THE GEMZ, Inc., a non-profit organization which mentors young ladies through personal development, leadership and youth entrepreneurship. Hundreds of teenage girls benefit from our work every year.

Even after all that, I experienced a phase in my life where I felt stagnant. I wasn't sure if I was on track with my goals and started experiencing anxiety. Sharing this with other women my age made me realize I was not alone. This realization became the launchpad for GENX LADIES, a lifestyle and professional community for hundreds of multicultural women 35 and over.

Your life's journey gives you a clue as to what your purpose is. Every experience you've ever had—whether it's pleasant or not so pleasant— is meant to be used to serve others. In your pursuit of purpose, take action. When you get a nudge to try something new, do it. Taking action regardless of your fears will lead to more clarity, which in turn will lead to a life of purpose. By honing in on your unique gifts and the value you provide and investing in developing yourself and your skills, you will find fulfillment and financial reward.

SUCCESS *Tips*

1. ALWAYS BELIEVE and be confident in your unique gifts and power. No one else can solve the problems and provide value the way you can.

2. IT IS OKAY TO REINVENT YOURSELF every so often; that's a sign of growth and evolution.

3. BUILD A PERSONAL AND PROFESSIONAL TEAM of people that are passionate, committed, and believe in your vision as much as you do.

august
SUCCESSES

1. _____
   _____
   _____

2. _____
   _____
   _____

3. _____
   _____
   _____

What I learned: _____
_____
_____
_____

How I'll celebrate my success: _____
_____
_____
_____

NOTES

NOTES

NOTES

SEPTEMBER

elle cole

Founder,
CleverlyChanging
@cleverlychanging

Ever since high school I'd wanted to go into law. I imagined myself arguing important cases and helping people with legal issues. A few years after receiving my undergraduate degrees in English and History, I became a paralegal and worked for a large television network. I thought my life was heading in the right direction. Then my husband and I found out we were having twins.

Having one child would have changed my plans slightly, but having twins meant I had to make some major adjustments. What was I going to do? Who would want to watch twin infants while I worked? My daughters were a few months old when I decided to quit my corporate job to raise them which, to me, was more important. This decision was not an easy one because I enjoyed my work and the extra income was helpful.

continued on page 96

Get it done

Review your vision and goals to make sure your actions this month align with the results you want.

ACTION	RESULTS
1.	
2.	
3.	

SEPTEMBER

S	M	T	W
		1	2
6	7	8	9
13	14	15	16
20	21	22	23
27	28	29	30

My goal as a wife and mom is to help my family thrive, not just win. Winning is temporary. Thriving is continual.

–ELLE COLE   #whoseshoes20

Th	F	S
3	4	5
10	11	12
17	18	19
24	25	26

IMPORTANT DATES

7 Labor Day
22 Autumn Begins

_____
_____
_____
_____
_____
_____
_____
_____
_____

AUGUST 2020

S	M	T	W	T	F	S
						1
2	3	4	5	6	7	8
9	10	11	12	13	14	15
16	17	18	19	20	21	22
23/30	24/31	25	26	27	28	29

OCTOBER 2020

S	M	T	W	T	F	S
				1	2	3
4	5	6	7	8	9	10
11	12	13	14	15	16	17
18	19	20	21	22	23	24
25	26	27	28	29	30	31

continued from page 92

I figured I would return to work once they were school age. However, my plans changed once again when one of my daughters was diagnosed with sickle cell anemia. A few years later, she was diagnosed with type 1 diabetes. My career was suddenly much less important than my daughter's health. Our doctor recommended homeschooling my daughters to help keep them both healthier. I knew I wouldn't be returning to work as I had planned.

Living on one income was challenging, but thankfully, I found a position where I could work virtually. I disciplined myself and paid off all of my student loans and debt and learned how to coupon to save money. I also got back into one of my hobbies: writing. My husband suggested I start a blog to share my experiences. Blogging was cathartic for me. At first, it felt like no one read my posts and that what I was doing was a waste of time. Over time, I realized my words had power and were helping mothers like me keep their kids healthy and educated. Almost a year after I started my blog, I received this message:

"Hey, I was reading another blog and discovered your blog. I have a 5 month old son with a diagnosis of sickle cell anemia. Like you, I was crushed. How is your daughter? How have you approached her diet and nutrition to keep her healthy and crisis-free? Thank you so much for responding!" Reading her words, I knew that I was not alone. Those words were the start of my community.

Although my life has not turned out as I planned, I'm able to share my knowledge and encouragement with thousands of people through my blog, speaking engagements, TV appearances, and podcast. I believe that sharing the wisdom God has given me is a gift: it is my purpose.

SUCCESS *Tips*

1. START BUILDING YOUR LEGACY TODAY. Don't wait for a tragedy to happen for you to impact the lives of others.

2. USE YOUR LIFE EXPERIENCES LIKE THEY ARE YOUR CLASSROOM because mistakes are okay.

3. YOUR PAST DOES NOT DETERMINE YOUR PATH, but your joy influences your journey!

september
SUCCESSES

1. _____
   _____
   _____

2. _____
   _____
   _____

3. _____
   _____
   _____

What I learned: _____
_____
_____
_____

How I'll celebrate my success: _____
_____
_____
_____

NOTES

NOTES

NOTES

_____

_____

_____

_____

_____

_____

_____

_____

_____

_____

_____

_____

_____

_____

_____

_____

_____

_____

_____

_____

_____

_____

_____

_____

OCTOBER

crystal swain-bates

Bestselling
Children's Author
@cswainbates

Ever since I was a little girl, I wanted to be a writer. Life took me in a lot of different, very fulfilling directions career-wise, but I still felt like something was missing. One day, I woke up with the crazy idea to quit my job working for the CIA. I decided I was going to start a publishing company and publish six books within one year. It was a very specific goal, yet I never doubted that I could achieve it. Once I make my mind up to do something, it's done, so I didn't look back or question my decision to leave

continued on page 106

Get it done

Review your vision and goals to make sure your actions this month align with the results you want.

ACTION	RESULTS
1.	
2.	
3.	

OCTOBER

S	M	T	W
4	5	6	7
11	12	13	14
18	19	20	21
25	26	27	28

Perfection is overrated. I'll take progress over perfection any day.

−CRYSTAL SWAIN-BATES   #whoseshoes20

Th	F	S
1	2	3
8	9	10
15	16	17
22	23	24
29	30	31

IMPORTANT DATES

12 Columbus Day

_____
_____
_____
_____
_____
_____
_____
_____

SEPTEMBER 2020

S	M	T	W	T	F	S
		1	2	3	4	5
6	7	8	9	10	11	12
13	14	15	16	17	18	19
20	21	22	23	24	25	26
27	28	29	30			

NOVEMBER 2020

S	M	T	W	T	F	S
1	2	3	4	5	6	7
8	9	10	11	12	13	14
15	16	17	18	19	20	21
22	23	24	25	26	27	28
29	30					

continued from page 102

my job. I simply looked at it as closing one chapter and starting a new one. However, once I put my plan into motion and started writing, fear started to creep in. I knew that I could write the books, but what would people think of them? Having always preferred to be behind the scenes, the thought of public rejection took me down the rabbit hole of self-doubt and fear. I even considered publishing my books under a different name so that people wouldn't know who I was.

My mom helped me remember something that fear and doubt had made me forget: my purpose. I wasn't publishing these books for myself. I was publishing them so that Black children around the world could read books with characters that looked like them. That goal was so much bigger than me or my fears.

I wrote down a long list of my whys: why I was writing these books; why they were important; why the world needed my gift; why my fear didn't matter. Once I finished, I knew that my reasons for pursuing my goal far exceeded any reasons I had not to. I published six books that year, and since then I have sold over 100,000 books, been featured in *Forbes* and *Essence*, and flown out to Amazon three time for my work filling the diversity gap in children's literature.

Overcoming my fears by surrounding them with all of my whys taught me the power of clarity. Once you are clear about what you want to accomplish, you become fearless.

SUCCESS *Tips*

1. JUST START WHERE YOU ARE, WITH WHAT YOU HAVE. Write the book. Start the blog. Record the podcast. Whatever ideas you've been sitting on, stop waiting for the perfect moment.

2. THERE IS NO GREATER INVESTMENT THAN THE ONE YOU MAKE IN YOURSELF. Instead of trying to figure everything out on your own, find someone who is where you want to be and invest in their courses or services to get the shortcut to success.

3. SURROUND YOURSELF WITH PEOPLE WHO GENUINELY WANT TO SEE YOU WIN and don't be afraid to make new friends.

october
SUCCESSES

1. _____

   _____

   _____

2. _____

   _____

   _____

3. _____

   _____

   _____

What I learned: _____

_____

_____

_____

How I'll celebrate my success: _____

_____

_____

_____

NOTES

NOTES

NOTES

NOVEMBER

k. denise hendershot

Speaker and Co-founder,
DiverseLuv Movement
@diverseluv

I grew up in a small town in Alabama with my grandparents. Black families lived on one side of the main street and white families lived on the other. At one point in my childhood, an exciting thing happened: a brand new Boys and Girls Club was built in our area. It was only a walk or bike ride away, but the quickest way to get there was to travel through my neighborhood, across the main street, and then through the White neighborhood.

The first time I rode my bike through the White neighborhood, I was met with

continued on page 116

Get it done

Review your vision and goals to make sure your actions this month align with the results you want.

ACTION	RESULTS
1.	
2.	
3.	

NOVEMBER

S	M	T	W
1	2	3	4
8	9	10	11
15	16	17	18
22	23	24	25
29	30		

As we remove the boundaries of how we luv and who we luv, we take the magic of luv to new heights. DiverseLuv is a movement, not a limitation – it's liberation. –K. DENISE HENDERSHOT   #whoseshoes20

Th	F	S
5	6	7
12	13	14
19	20	21
26	27	28

IMPORTANT DATES

1 Daylight Saving Time Ends

11 Veterans Day

26 Thanksgiving

_____
_____
_____
_____
_____
_____
_____

OCTOBER 2020

S	M	T	W	T	F	S
				1	2	3
4	5	6	7	8	9	10
11	12	13	14	15	16	17
18	19	20	21	22	23	24
25	26	27	28	29	30	31

DECEMBER 2020

S	M	T	W	T	F	S
		1	2	3	4	5
6	7	8	9	10	11	12
13	14	15	16	17	18	19
20	21	22	23	24	25	26
27	28	29	30	31		

continued from page 112

hatred in the form of rocks being thrown at me and venomous yelling: "N****r, go back to your neighborhood!" I felt, at that moment, my spirit was completely broken. Then I remembered: I had to go back through there to get home! I was met with the same treatment on the way home.

I was often the only one to take that chance to ride through that neighborhood. Most of the other Black kids took the long way around. But I believed that I belonged to that community so I had the right to ride through. That was a defining time for me. I remember thinking, at every given opportunity, I wanted to make people feel like they belonged, like they were included, and that their presence mattered.

From then to now, I have been "the only" in more situations than I can count. The only Black person on a business team; the only Black person on a sports team; the only female on a team; the only Black person in a meeting, and the list goes on. To say I was uncomfortable in those situations is an understatement.

So how does someone with these types of stories grow up and enter into an interracial marriage? I simply didn't allow my past experiences to determine my future. Committed to finding ways to foster a spirit of inclusion in the world we live in, my husband and I started a movement called DiverseLuv and are working on a book to share our experiences and knowledge on love and diversity. Through it all, I have learned to love who God sets before me—despite our differences.

SUCCESS *Tips*

1. **PERSONAL LOVE:** Do something daily that allows you to fall in love with yourself over and over again.

2. **PROJECTED LOVE:** Evaluate what you love about your spouse, family, friends, associates, and community and ensure that your love is authentic and reciprocated in some healthy form.

3. **PROFESSIONAL LOVE:** Take time to learn the love language of the different circles in which you network. Be a resource, but also learn to accept the resources God sends your way.

november
SUCCESSES

1. _____
   _____
   _____

2. _____
   _____
   _____

3. _____
   _____
   _____

What I learned: _____
_____
_____
_____

How I'll celebrate my success: _____
_____
_____
_____

NOTES

NOTES

NOTES

_____

_____

_____

_____

_____

_____

_____

_____

_____

_____

_____

_____

_____

_____

_____

_____

_____

_____

_____

_____

_____

_____

_____

DECEMBER

dr. vikki johnson

Founder,
SOUL WEALTH,
Authentic Living
Enterprises LLC
@allthingsvikki

For years I chased the wrong things to fill a void in me; it became a habit that created a cycle of co-dependency. I found myself in relationships that were filled with passion, yet unhealthy for my soul. I had mastered the art of emotional manipulation. At the end of it all, however, my soul was depleted. I was fed up with being in relationships with men who were mentally or emotionally unavailable. I was going through life on fumes and frustrated. I now know I was emotionally unavailable myself and attracted the same in my

continued on page 126

Get it done

Review your vision and goals to make sure your actions this month align with the results you want.

ACTION	RESULTS
1.	
2.	
3.	

DECEMBER

S	M	T	W
		1	2
6	7	8	9
13	14	15	16
20	21	22	23
27	28	29	30

In every moment, we live at choice.

–DR. VIKKI JOHNSON   #whoseshoes20

Th	F	S
3	4	5
10	11	12
17	18	19
24	25	26
31		

IMPORTANT DATES

21 Winter Begins
24 Christmas Eve
25 Christmas Day
31 New Year's Eve

_____
_____
_____
_____
_____
_____
_____
_____

NOVEMBER 2020

S	M	T	W	T	F	S
1	2	3	4	5	6	7
8	9	10	11	12	13	14
15	16	17	18	19	20	21
22	23	24	25	26	27	28
29	30					

JANUARY 2021

S	M	T	W	T	F	S
					1	2
3	4	5	6	7	8	9
10	11	12	13	14	15	16
17	18	19	20	21	22	23
24/31	25	26	27	28	29	30

continued from page 122

life because I consistently betrayed what my heart and soul really wanted. I was committed to pleasing other people. I know what it is to sacrifice what I want so other people will be okay. I know what it is to settle for less than I desire or deserve. I know what it is to be in a relationship that does not feel good to me. I've had to learn some emotionally expensive lessons.

After my second abortion, I was at my emotional bottom and tired of being exhausted. During this time, I had the courage to ask myself some very real questions: What was I doing? Where was my life headed? Why was I doing the things I was doing? How did I get here? I heard the answer in a quiet whisper: *Life is all about getting the lessons while on the journey. It is about the journey, Vikki, not the destination.* After this realization, I started saying "yes" to what I deeply wanted and became more courageous. I also put distance between me and anything or anyone toxic. I started making healthier choices that lit up my soul.

Our wounds are our best teachers. If we are willing to learn, we become wiser after recovering from each broken place. The truth is, we can't give away what we don't have. We also attract what we reflect. If we are discontent, nothing outside of ourselves will automatically settle our soul. We must get to know who we are in the most intimate way. Surprisingly, most of us are not in touch with ourselves enough to know what we have to offer the world because we're so busy fixing others.

My favorite question to ask other women is, "Would you want to be in a relationship with *you*?" Regardless of the answer, you must practice loving *you*! Practice being a good, loyal friend to the person in the mirror. Your soul is worthy of wealth *right now*. You are enough *right now*. When you make *you* a priority then the world will do the same.

SUCCESS *Tips*

1. BE FULLY PRESENT IN EVERY MOMENT.

2. YOU DON'T *HAVE* TO DO ANYTHING, so choose wisely as to who you allow to have access to you.

3. LIVE FROM YOUR OVERFLOW and not your capacity so you don't function from a place of deficiency.

december

SUCCESSES

1. _____
_____
_____

2. _____
_____
_____

3. _____
_____
_____

What I learned: _____
_____
_____
_____

How I'll celebrate my success: _____
_____
_____
_____

NOTES

NOTES

NOTES

believe in yourself

CHRISTINE ST. VIL

"Believe in yourself and all that you are. Know that there is something inside of you greater than any obstacle."

–CHRISTIAN D. LARSON

Believe you are more than the limits that society may place on you. Believe you are more than just a pretty face. Believe you are more than your past hurts, your past pains, and your past mistakes. Believe that you are more. And don't let anyone tell you otherwise!

Believe you are perfect for what God created you to be and do. Know that you were created in His image. His image is always perfect. His image is never a mistake.

Believe that you belong in those rooms. Believe that you deserve those opportunities. Because you do. We see you. Do you see you?

This year, we want you to remember and believe that:

You Belong. Period.

You Earned it. Period.

You Deserve it. Period.

You are Capable. Period.

You are Loved. Period.

Queen: You are a Fighter. A conqueror. A Believer. They will try to destroy you with their words. But don't give them that power. You have to be able to look in the mirror and tell yourself how much you love yourself.

Your vision becomes your thoughts. Your thoughts become your words. Your words become your actions. Your actions become your reality.

Be confident in your brilliance. Hold your head up high. Surround yourself with more believers. Live in the moment and celebrate even what you consider to be small successes.

2020 is the year of vision. And with vision, comes light. Don't allow anyone to dim your light. The world needs you. Even when you're feeling alone, you are not alone. Read these words until you believe them for yourself. You matter. Your. Life. Matters. Don't ever forget that. Your past mistakes do not define you, they only make you stronger.

Beautiful Queen, you are more than what's on the surface. You are light to someone else's darkness. You are happiness to someone else's sadness. You are magnificent, just the way God created you to be.

Remember these three simple steps to achieving success:

ASK. It's as simple as asking God for what you want.

BELIEVE. Once you make the ask, you've got to believe with all your heart that it can be done (the how is not important here).

RECEIVE. Prepare to receive what you ask for; get things in line and act as though you've already received it.

You are what you believe. So we hope that this year, you will believe in YOU. Because we believe in you.

Cheers to your 2020 Vision,

Love,

Christine and Julian

Believe

in your ability.

NOTES

NOTES

NOTES

NOTES

NOTES

NOTES

NOTES

NOTES

NOTES

NOTES

NOTES

NOTES

2O21 *Calendar*

JANUARY

S	M	T	W	T	F	S
					1	2
3	4	5	6	7	8	9
10	11	12	13	14	15	16
17	18	19	20	21	22	23
$^{24}/_{31}$	25	26	27	28	29	30

FEBRUARY

S	M	T	W	T	F	S
	1	2	3	4	5	6
7	8	9	10	11	12	13
14	15	16	17	18	19	20
21	22	23	24	25	26	27
28						

MARCH

S	M	T	W	T	F	S
	1	2	3	4	5	6
7	8	9	10	11	12	13
14	15	16	17	18	19	20
21	22	23	24	25	26	27
28	29	30	31			

APRIL

S	M	T	W	T	F	S
				1	2	3
4	5	6	7	8	9	10
11	12	13	14	15	16	17
18	19	20	21	22	23	24
25	26	27	28	29	30	

MAY

S	M	T	W	T	F	S
						1
2	3	4	5	6	7	8
9	10	11	12	13	14	15
16	17	18	19	20	21	22
$^{23}/_{30}$	$^{24}/_{31}$	25	26	27	28	29

JUNE

S	M	T	W	T	F	S
		1	2	3	4	5
6	7	8	9	10	11	12
13	14	15	16	17	18	19
20	21	22	23	24	25	26
27	28	29	30			

JULY

S	M	T	W	T	F	S
				1	2	3
4	5	6	7	8	9	10
11	12	13	14	15	16	17
18	19	20	21	22	23	24
25	26	27	28	29	30	31

AUGUST

S	M	T	W	T	F	S
1	2	3	4	5	6	7
8	9	10	11	12	13	14
15	16	17	18	19	20	21
22	23	24	25	26	27	28
29	30	31				

SEPTEMBER

S	M	T	W	T	F	S
			1	2	3	4
5	6	7	8	9	10	11
12	13	14	15	16	17	18
19	20	21	22	23	24	25
26	27	28	29	30		

OCTOBER

S	M	T	W	T	F	S
					1	2
3	4	5	6	7	8	9
10	11	12	13	14	15	16
17	18	19	20	21	22	23
$^{24}/_{31}$	25	26	27	28	29	30

NOVEMBER

S	M	T	W	T	F	S
	1	2	3	4	5	6
7	8	9	10	11	12	13
14	15	16	17	18	19	20
21	22	23	24	25	26	27
28	29	30				

DECEMBER

S	M	T	W	T	F	S
			1	2	3	4
5	6	7	8	9	10	11
12	13	14	15	16	17	18
19	20	21	22	23	24	25
26	27	28	29	30	31	

THE TEAM
Behind the Planner

CHRISTINE ST.VIL is a wife, mother of three, speaker, writer, author and trainer. She is relentless about helping women, particularly moms, take charge of their lives by learning how to feel good without feeling guilty. Through her work with Moms 'N Charge™, Purpose Driven Media™ was created to teach women entrepreneurs how to successfully leverage social media and blogging to start and/or grow their business and brand. Christine is an instructor in the Steve Harvey RADICAL Success Institute and her work has been featured in numerous local and national TV and online media outlets including VOA, Fox 5 DC, Fox 45, WBAL, WHUR, AllParenting.com, Sirius XM, and others. She received her B.S. in biology from Marymount University.

  @MomsNCharge @PDMediaGroup

web: www.momsncharge.com, www.socialscoopgroup.com

JULIAN B. KIGANDA is a transformational brand strategist, award-winning graphic designer, and accomplished speaker who specializes in building inclusive brands for clients ranging from Fortune 500 corporations to multimillion-dollar nonprofit organizations and small businesses. As CEO of JBK Brand Design, her expertise in design, branding, marketing, and communications have helped her clients land multi-million dollar sponsors, sell out events, and increase product sales by 800% overnight. A voice of authority in her industry, Julian has taught branding and marketing courses at Bowie State University and has been a featured speaker at the United Nations, NAACP Convention, the Motion Picture Association of America, and Georgetown University. She's been featured in numerous media outlets, including ABC News, *The Washington Post*, Essence.com, *ARISE* magazine, Voice of America and NPR. She received her B.A. in graphic design from Marymount University.

  @JulianBKiganda @jbkbranddesign

web: www.jbkbranddesign.com

About the book

Do you find yourself living the definition of insanity on a daily basis? Is it hard for you to say "no" to people, things, and situations that drain you? Are you allowing unhealthy relationships to block your blessings? Do you struggle to reconcile your cultural heritage with the woman you want to become? Are you still waiting for Prince Charming to come along and complete you before you can really be happy?

If you answered "yes" to any of these questions, then *you need this book*. Julian B. Kiganda and Christine K. St. Vil are two sisters known for being Bold & Fearless Moms 'N Charge. After conquering their own personal and professional struggles to finally walk in their purpose, they're giving you their most powerful insights to move you along your own path to uncovering your God-given purpose. In *Whose Shoes Are You Wearing?*, these no-nonsense siblings take you through key steps to help you create the unprecedented transformation you want to see in your own life. They draw upon their own life-changing experiences—from ending unhealthy relationships to surviving unimaginable trauma—which are closely intertwined with their East African upbringing. With practical action steps included at the end of each chapter, *Whose Shoes* shows you how to walk boldly and fearlessly in your own shoes, regardless of the shoes you've been wearing.

With a generous dose of humor, solid spiritual principles, and a "keepin' it real" attitude, this book will become a staple in your library as you embark upon your own journey to discover the shoes God meant for you!

AVAILABLE ONLINE AT MAHOGANYBOOKS.COM, AMAZON AND BARNES & NOBLE

Whose Shoes Are YOU WEARING?

40+ AMAZON REVIEWS

Whose Shoes Are You Wearing? is an excellent book for anyone, regardless of gender, who wants to understand the value of discovering, accepting and fully loving self to establish a rock-solid foundation for healthy relationships and fulfilling lives of passion and purpose. Whose Shoes will inspire you to step out on faith and onto the path of your choosing."
—ALFRED A. EDMOND, JR., SVP/Chief Content Officer, *Black Enterprise;* Co-author, *Loving in the Grown Zone: A No-Nonsense Guide to Making Healthy Decisions in the Quest for Loving, Romantic Relationships of Honor, Esteem and Respect* (Balboa Press)

"I absolutely loved this book. Christine St. Vil and Julian Kiganda have redefined self-help. I laughed and cried while reading this book. This is a must read . . . Julian and Christine share their personal stories so freely, but yet tie it back to a lesson that will help you grow. There is something for everyone. Highly recommend!" —AT

"After reading this book, I felt empowered to be flawed! It sounds a little crazy, but this book was such a refreshing look at how being exactly who you are is all that you are called to do in this world . . . Julian's story was so honest and revealing that if you've ever struggled with relationships and dating, you really need to get this book. If you have a problem saying 'no' Christine says 'No' is a complete sentence (go straight to Chapter 6) . . . I'm happy I got my hands on this book." —QUEENIE

"I would recommend this [book] to anyone (women/men alike) who is willing to do the work to find the right fit of shoes, even if the process of getting fitted and trying on several other shoes is frustrating and unsuccessful initially. Read this book and walk in your own shoes!" —DE'NITA MOSS

5 stars!

Photo credits

Page 12: Jazmin Buford

Page 22: Santos Paris Photography

Page 32: Topia Tessema

Page 42: Tora Carter

Page 52: Devon Warren Photography

Page 62: Dawn Smith

Page 72: Teresa Alvarez

Page 82: VSDavis Photography

Page 92: David Cavins

Page 102: Ace of 360 Photos

Page 122: C-Suite Pics

Pages 2, 148, 149: EvvettMarcell Photography

Join our mailing list at
www.whoseshoesbook.com

To place additional orders of this planner, visit bit.ly/orderwsbplanner2020. For bulk pricing, contact us at info@whoseshoesbook.com.

FOLLOW US ON SOCIAL MEDIA

Twitter @whoseshoesbook

Instagram @whoseshoesbook

@whoseshoesbook

YouTube www.youtube.com/whoseshoesbook